Ancient EGYPT

JANE SHUTER

WAYLAND

History Beneath Your Feet

Titles in this series

Ancient Egypt
Ancient Greece

Editor: Jonathan Ingoldby
Series design: Christopher Halls at Mind's Eye Design
Illustrations: John Yates
Project artwork: John Yates
Production controller: Carol Stevens
Consultant: Dr Joann Fletcher, BA, Ph.D.

First published in Great Britain in 1999 by
Wayland (Publishers) Ltd,
Reprinted in 2000 by Wayland,
an imprint of Hachette Children's Books
This paperback edition published in 2003
Reprinted in 2004
Re-issued in 2008

Wayland
338 Euston Road, London NW1 3BH
Wayland is a division of Hachette Children's
Books, an Hachette Livre UK Company

British Library Cataloguing in Publication Data
Shuter, Jane
 Ancient Egypt. - (History beneath your feet)
 1. Egypt - Antiquities - Juvenile literature 2. Egypt -
Civilization - To 332 B.C. - Juvenile literature 3. Egypt
- Civilization - 332 B.C. - 638 A.D. - Juvenile literature
I. Title
932

ISBN 978-0-7502-5399-4

Printed in China

Cover photographs: Robert Harding (the 'Bent
Pyramid' at Dahshur; Tutankhamun's death mask)

The publishers would like to thank the following for
permission to publish their pictures (t=top; c=centre;
b=bottom; l=left; r=right)

AKG (London) 4–5, 18, 27, 32, 33, 43; The Ancient
Egypt Picture Library 13bl, 13br, 34, 35, 38, 39; The
Bridgeman Art Library London 6; C.M. Dixon 12, 22,
31, 36; Joann Fletcher 5 br, 8bl, 17, 24, 37, 41; Robert
Harding 7, 11c, 14–15, 28, 29; Michael Holford 10, 16,
19, 30; Norma Joseph 40; Science Photo Library 23, 42;
University of Manchester/Richard Neave 25; Wayland
Picture Library 11tr, 20, 22, 26

All Wayland books encourage children to read and help them improve their literacy.

 The contents page, page numbers, headings and index help locate specific pieces of information.

 The glossary reinforces alphabetic knowledge and extends vocabulary.

 The further information section suggests other books dealing with the same subject.

 Find out more about how this book is specifically relevant to the National Literacy Strategy on page 47.

CONTENTS

WHAT IS ARCHAEOLOGY?

'Archaeology' is a Greek word meaning 'the study of ancient things'. Archaeologists study the remains of people, buildings and objects from earlier times and then piece together what life had been like in the past. Some of these remains are so old that they have become hidden by earth or more recent buildings. This means that archaeologists first have to find where these remains are hidden, and then dig down or 'excavate' to see what is there. This is why so much history is 'beneath your feet'.

WHO WERE THE ANCIENT EGYPTIANS?

The ancient Egyptians lived along the banks of the River Nile. Once a year, the Nile flooded, leaving deposits of fertile mud, where crops could be grown. Because there was never any rain, the rest of Egypt was desert; nothing could grow there.

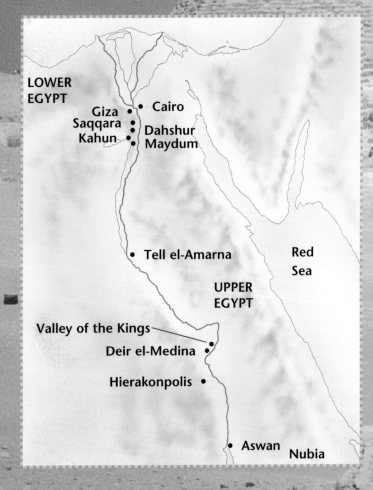

LOWER EGYPT

Giza
Saqqara
Kahun
Cairo
Dahshur
Maydum

Tell el-Amarna

Red Sea

UPPER EGYPT

Valley of the Kings
Deir el-Medina

Hierakonpolis

Aswan   Nubia

At first Egypt was divided into two countries: Upper and Lower Egypt. In about 3000 BC these were united and ruled by a pharaoh (king), until Egypt was taken over by the Romans in 30 BC.

The ancient Egyptians are famous for their pyramids, temples and beautifully painted tombs. They are also famous for their method of preserving their dead: mummification.

Most of the evidence about ancient Egyptian life comes from their burials because the ancient Egyptians believed in life after death. So they preserved the body of the dead person and buried them with many of their possessions, for use in the afterlife. People were buried with care and in tombs that were made to last.

The most famous tombs of all – the pyramids of Giza.

This Egyptologist is brushing the sand off a skull. He is taking great care, so as not to damage it.

Modern archaeologists specializing in the study of ancient Egypt are called Egyptologists. They study the remains of pyramids, temples, tombs and towns still to be found in Egypt. They also study written records and artefacts that have survived.

Because Egypt has an arid (desert) climate, ancient artefacts have been preserved well. For example, wood does not rot if it is buried in the hot, dry sand. As a result, wooden ploughs and other farming tools have been found, which otherwise would have rotted away long ago.

EARLY ARCHAEOLOGY IN EGYPT

Today, Egyptologists who wish to excavate in Egypt must have permission from the government. They have to explain what they are looking for, and agree to give the government anything that they find. Modern Egyptologists are highly trained professionals who know how to excavate carefully and always keep detailed records so that others can understand what has been found. Early 'archaeology' was nothing like this.

'The Antiques Seller', painted by C. Wilda in 1884. At this time local people regularly raided tombs and made a living selling the artefacts they found.

TOMB RAIDERS

The first 'archaeologists' were little more than tomb raiders: treasure hunters out to plunder tombs for profit. As a result, very few kept records of what they found or where they had been, and anything they discovered that could not easily be sold was thrown away as 'worthless'.

Some of these fortune hunters were wealthy already: they could afford their journey to Egypt, and were able to pay local workers to do the digging for them. Others worked on rich people's behalf, who paid their expenses, sometimes for many years, in the hope they would discover an untouched tomb full of treasure.

THE STRONGMAN OF ARCHAEOLOGY

Giovanni Belzoni was a circus strongman who went to Egypt in 1814 when he was 37, trying to sell the Egyptians a new kind of waterwheel. He failed, but while he was there he saw how much money could be made from selling 'ancient treasures'. He discovered six royal tombs and excavated several temples, and as a result Egyptian treasures became very fashionable in Europe. Unlike many of his competitors, he did take some care with his excavations, and even drew maps, one of which records where some of the statues he plundered had once stood.

This 1816 painting by Belzoni records the removal of the head of Rameses II from Thebes. It took 110 workers a whole day to move the head 70 metres.

EARLY BURIALS

Egyptologists have discovered human remains in the desert which show that the earliest Egyptians were buried directly into the hot desert sand. The bodies have been preserved because the sand soaked up all the bodily fluids. The scientific technique of radiocarbon dating revealed one of these bodies to be about 5,000 years old.

Later, burials became more complicated. People buried their dead in brick-lined pits, baskets or wooden coffins. Without contact with the sand to soak up the fluids, the bodies rotted away. Because preservation of the body was important for the passage to the afterlife, the ancient Egyptians had to discover a method of preservation that was as good, or better, than sand.

These Egyptologists are excavating an early burial at Hierakonpolis, 80 kilometres south of Luxor.

RADIOCARBON DATING

Archaeologists use radiocarbon dating to find out how old the bodies they discover are. All living things contain carbon, which they absorb, day by day. When they die, they stop absorbing carbon. The remaining carbon then begins to decay, and the rate of this decay can be measured in a laboratory on a specially designed machine. The lower the carbon count, the older the body.

PROJECT: PRESERVATION EXPERIMENT

You will need:
Four glass jars, with lids (jam-jars are ideal)
Enough sand to fill the first jar
Enough mud to fill the second jar
Enough water to fill the third jar
An apple

1. Cut the apple into quarters.
2. Half fill the first jar with sand, the second with mud and the third with water. Put a piece of the apple into each jar so that part of it is visible through the glass, but not squashed against it. Fill each jar to the top.
3. Put the last piece of apple into the fourth jar with nothing around it but air.
4. Put the lids on the jars, and store them somewhere safe, in the sun.
5. Leave the jars for two days and then examine the apple in each. Is the same thing happening to all the pieces?
6. Look again after a week: what has happened?

FLINDERS PETRIE

Sir Flinders Petrie (1853–1942) discovered the arm of the first royal mummy, King Zer, in a royal tomb which had been 'ransacked' (as he put it) by earlier treasure-hunting 'archaeologists'. Petrie began archaeological work in Egypt in 1880, and made many other very important discoveries, including Tell el-Amarna (see page 35). He spent more than 40 years in Egypt and the Middle East, and was the first to use many archaeological techniques which are still used today. He was one of the first archaeologists to see the importance of 'stratification' – digging down carefully, layer by layer – because each layer comes from a different point in the past. The deeper you dig, the further back you go in time. Rushed digging can jumble up the evidence.

'Stratification': usually, the deeper an object is buried, the older it is.

9

PYRAMIDS

For almost 1,000 years the ancient Egyptians built pyramids as places to bury their pharaohs. Even the smallest of them are huge. Egyptologists have had to piece together clues to find out how these massive structures were built using only the simplest of tools.

HOW DID THE PYRAMIDS GET THEIR SHAPE?

If you look at the earliest pyramids you can work out how the famous, later pyramids got their shape.

The first stone pyramid is the Step Pyramid at Saqqara, which has a square base and goes up in steps. As pyramid design developed, pyramids came to have smooth sides, which were covered with a layer of limestone and polished until they shone.

Egyptologists examined a smooth-sided pyramid at Maydum, which had worn away to show the inside. They saw that it had been built as a step pyramid, and the steps had been filled in to make the sides smooth. This is likely to be the way all smooth-sided pyramids were made.

The Step Pyramid at Saqqara, built in the reign of Djoser. It originally had six steps and was 60 metres high.

IMHOTEP, ROYAL ARCHITECT

The pharaoh Djoser (2668–2649 BC) employed the architect Imhotep to design the Step Pyramid. Imhotep was also Djoser's vizier (the highest official in the land) and his doctor. His skills and reputation were so great that 2,000 years after his death Imhotep had come to be regarded as a god, an honour usually reserved for the pharaohs alone. We know about Imhotep from written records and from statues discovered by archaeologists which show him as a god.

A statue of Imhotep as a god. He was worshipped as the god of knowledge, writing and medicine.

BUILDING A PYRAMID

First the ground was levelled to make a flat surface. Despite the huge area covered by the Great Pyramid at Giza (you could fit over 200 tennis courts into its base), the level of the ground varies by less than 2.5 centimetres from one side to the other. Such precision was essential because even a small difference at ground level would cause huge problems to the structure as the pyramid rose.

Early pyramid builders did not always get things right. The 'Bent Pyramid' at Dahshur changes its angle halfway up. Egyptologists have concluded that the builders realized the pyramid would be too high and thin if they carried on building it at the original angle of 54 degrees, and would not be strong enough to support itself. They did not want to undo all their years of hard work, so they simply changed the angle to 43 degrees, allowing the pyramid to meet at its point much sooner.

The 'Bent Pyramid' at Dahshur, built in the reign of Sneferu. This pyramid is not only unusual because of its shape, but also for having two entrances instead of the usual one.

HOW DID THEY MOVE ALL THAT HEAVY STONE?

Ancient Egyptian mathematical writings show that they knew how to make stable pyramids. However, early archaeologists could only guess at how the Egyptians built such huge structures from heavy stone using only simple tools.

Bit by bit, evidence emerged: wooden rollers were found near the pyramid site at Lahun, and a tomb painting was discovered which showed workers moving a huge statue on a wooden platform using rollers. The platform was hauled along with ropes. It is thought that the blocks of stone used in pyramid building were moved in this way and then levered into position after rolling them up an earth bank.

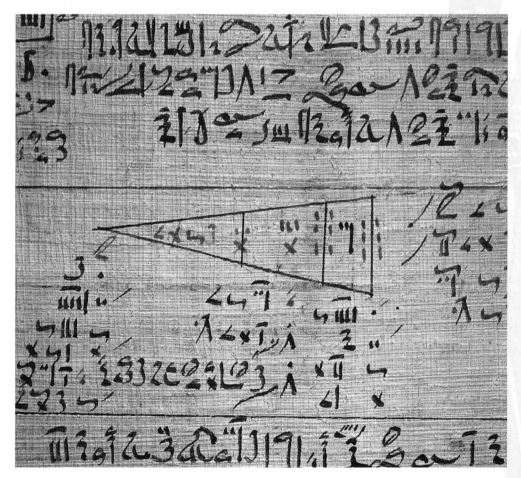

Part of the Rhind Mathematical Papyrus, written about 1650 BC, but said to be a copy of a text written much earlier.

THE PYRAMID COMPLEX

Remains discovered around pyramids show that they did not stand on their own but were part of a walled-in complex of buildings. The pyramid was usually built on high ground, with a temple beside it where priests performed rituals for the dead pharaoh. A walled road led from this temple to one or more other temples in the valley. There were also smaller pyramids for the royal family and simpler tombs for important officials. The closer to the pharaoh's pyramid these structures were, the more important the person buried inside them would have been.

THE REAL FACE OF THE SPHINX?

A statue of the pharaoh Khafra.

The Sphinx was built by the pharaoh Khafra, who ruled from 2558–2532 BC, and also built the second of the three pyramids of Giza. His pyramid complex was impressive, and although his pyramid was slightly smaller than his father's (the Great Pyramid of Cheops), he sited it on higher ground to make it look bigger! Within his pyramid complex Khafra had the famous Sphinx constructed, and Egyptologists believe that the face of the Sphinx is a likeness of the pharaoh.

The face of the Sphinx.

THE VALLEY OF THE KINGS

The Valley of the Kings is a long, narrow valley in western Thebes, where nearly all the pharaohs from 1524–1070 BC were buried. So far, nearly 100 tombs have been discovered. Some are pharaoh's tombs, others belong to members of the royal family and important court officials.

Because the tombs were built for important people, they were filled with splendid and expensive furniture, clothes and jewellery, as well as food and other belongings. Because of this, the tombs have always attracted robbers. Almost all had been broken into and their valuable goods stolen before they were discovered by Egyptologists. However, what remained has helped Egyptologists to build up a picture of ancient Egyptian life.

The Valley of the Kings today.

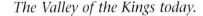

THEODORE DAVIS

Theodore Davis (1837–1915) was a rich American whose first excavations in the Valley of the Kings began in 1903. Davis's team found many tombs, mostly robbed of their precious contents. However there were still wall paintings, mummies and less valuable artefacts to study. In 1912 Davis gave up excavating, sure that there was nothing left to find. Within 2 metres of where he stopped work was the entrance to the one tomb in the valley that had not been robbed of its treasure: the tomb of Tutankhamun.

GROUND PENETRATION RADAR

If only the archaeologists who excavated the Valley of the Kings had had ground penetration radar. The antenna of this equipment sends high frequency radio waves into the earth. When the radio waves are blocked – by an object or even a change from soil to rock – they bounce back.

A computer stores this information and allows archaeologists to create 'maps' of what lies under the earth without having to dig at all. The radar can tell the difference between metal, wood, stone and brick and can even detect air-filled spaces.

INSIDE THE TOMBS

TOMB PAINTINGS

Because they have not been exposed to very much light, Egyptian tomb paintings glow with colour even after thousands of years. They were painted for the dead, but they can tell Egyptologists a lot about the living, as long as they remember that the paintings show the afterlife. The afterlife was just like everyday life, with one important difference: it was supposed to be perfect, and tomb artists were meant to follow strict rules to make sure they showed perfection.

The tomb artists hardly ever painted people as ugly, deformed, or even old. They rarely showed pregnant women, because pregnancy was a dangerous time for women. Nor did they show famine or poverty. The rivers they painted were always teeming with fish and water birds to hunt. The fields were always full of crops, and the tomb owner and his family harvested or hunted in their best clothes!

Ancient Egyptian artists had to follow other rules when they painted the tombs. For example, the size of people in the pictures was related to their importance, not their real size, so that the tomb owner was the largest figure, and his or her servants the smallest.

This tomb painting, from about 1400 BC, shows the tomb owner hunting in the afterlife. The painter has made sure that there are plenty of birds and fish to catch. Note that the daughter is painted much smaller than the tomb owner or his wife.

CHEMICAL ANALYSIS

The ancient Egyptians were the first people to invent and use an artificial paint to create a special shade of blue used in their tomb decoration. Archaeologists found this out by taking small flakes of paint from the tombs and analysing them to find out what they were made from. Instead of the expected natural ingredients, such as crushed plants or rocks, they found a mixture of copper, calcium and silica (sand), which had been heated to very high temperatures to create the colour.

PROJECT: A TOMB PAINTING

Imagine you were an artist doing a wall painting for the pharaoh's tomb, using the same designs as the ancient Egyptians. Look at the wall paintings shown in this book for ideas. Work on smooth cardboard if possible, because it is a more 'wall-like' surface than paper.

1. Paint the cardboard white.

2. While it dries, sketch the scene you want to show on a piece of scrap paper, so that you know how much space each part will take up.

3. Draw a grid of 1 centimetre squares over your sketch using red crayon or pencil, and another grid of 3 centimetre squares on the cardboard. Make the grid as faint as possible, but make sure you can see it.

4. Copy your sketch onto the wall, enlarging things by using the grids.

5. Paint the picture. If you did not press too hard when making your grid, the paint will cover it up.

This wall painting was not completed, so you can still see the grid lines.

GRAVE GOODS

Because the ancient Egyptians buried their dead with all the things they thought they would need in the afterlife, Egyptologists have found clothes, jewellery, wigs, make-up, furniture, household equipment, toys, weapons and even chariots and boats. *Shabtis* were also buried with the dead person. These were models representing servants, who would work for them in the afterlife.

A tomb model showing servants making beer.

The grave goods that really bring ancient Egypt to life are the tomb models. These show all kinds of everyday activity: baking, weaving, fishing, sailing and even beermaking. They show buildings too, such as granaries, houses and gardens.

BEERMAKING IN ANCIENT EGYPT

Egyptologists have used several kinds of evidence to work out how the ancient Egyptians made beer. Tomb models and paintings show that beer was made by dissolving bread in water flavoured with honey, dates or spices. This mixture was left for a few days and then strained into fresh jars.

The remains at the bottom of these jars show that the 'beer' was weak and quite thick. The remains of a reed drinking straw have also been found, used to filter out some of the sediment. Egyptologists were not sure what the straw was for until they discovered a painting showing a man using one to drink his beer.

BOATS OF THE DEAD

Boat models were included in almost every burial, so that the dead person could travel to the afterlife. Models and paintings of boats show archaeologists how ancient Egyptian boats were rigged, their general shape and how they were crewed. They do not show actual measurements because they are often out of proportion.

However, a find in 1954 revealed that pharaohs had real boats buried near them. A 'boat pit' was discovered by the Great Pyramid, containing a boat that had been dismantled for burial. The pieces were removed and treated with chemicals to stop them rotting. Archaeologists then began to piece the boat together like a jigsaw. It took several attempts before they got it right!

A tomb model of a funeral boat from a Middle Kingdom tomb. These boats were small, and as they only made short journeys they did not need a sail or many crew.

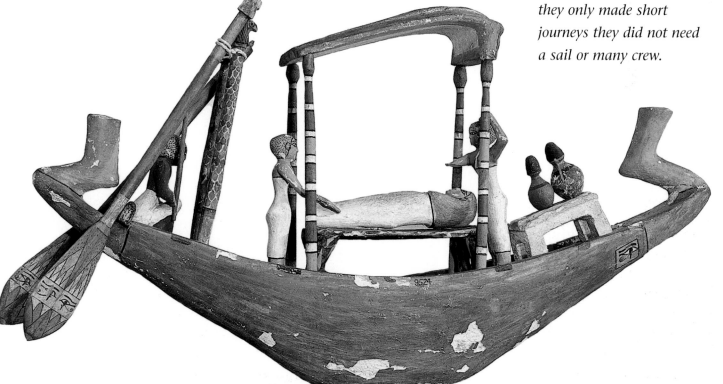

THE MYSTERY OF HIEROGLYPHS

From the very first, Egyptologists were fascinated by ancient Egyptian writing. Hieroglyphs (meaning 'sacred writing') is the name used to describe the picture-writing most commonly found in tombs and on official documents, walls, mummy cases, *shabtis* and statues. But what did hieroglyphs say?

The Rosetta Stone, with hieroglyphs at the top, demotic in the centre and Greek at the bottom.

Egyptologists knew that there were two forms of writing in ancient Egypt: hieroglyphs and hieratic writing, which was a simplified version of hieroglyphs, used for everyday documents. But they could not work out how to read either form. It was a code they had no idea how to crack.

Then, in 1799, a slab of stone was discovered which had the same text on it in Greek, a later form of hieratic called demotic, and hieroglyphs. This was the Rosetta Stone, the key to deciphering hieroglyphic writing. However, even with the Stone, the task was very hard. Demotic text was understood first, because it was more like a conventional alphabet. Hieroglyphic writing took much longer: about 25 years.

JEAN FRANÇOIS CHAMPOLLION: THE CODEBREAKER

Jean François Champollion (1790–1832) was the Frenchman who cracked the hieroglyph code. In 1822 he said he could understand some hieroglyphs. It took him 10 more years to work out the grammar and produce a word list. He was helped in this huge task by Egyptologists who carefully copied the inscriptions they found so that he could study as many examples as possible.

WHAT HIEROGLYPHS SAY

The hieroglyphs in royal tombs and temples often listed the titles of the pharaoh, his great achievements and even the amount of grain he gave out each year. This may seem rather dull, although it is valuable information for Egyptologists. Sometimes, though, hieroglyphs act as 'speech bubbles' for the people in a painting or carving. An example of this is shown below.

A cartoon of two Egyptian labourers working in the fields, based on a wall painting in the tomb of Sonebi. The speech bubbles give a rough translation of the hieroglyphs.

MUMMIES

Mummies are the bodies of the dead which have been preserved using the process of embalming. Embalmers took out most of the internal organs from the body, and then dried the body in *natron*, a kind of salt. They removed the brain by hooking it out through the nose.

When the *natron* had absorbed all the fluids from the body (just as sand had done in the early burials), it was filled with linen and spices, and sewn up again. It was then wrapped in strips of linen. New linen was mostly used for pharaohs and other important people, but old clothes or sheets were used for ordinary people.

A painting showing the jackal-headed god of the dead, Anubis, preparing a mummy.

It took about 350 square metres of cloth to wrap the average mummy, the equivalent of about 200 large bedsheets! Tucked into the bandages at different layers were amulets to protect the dead person from evil.

Because people found mummies so fascinating in the nineteenth century, some were unwrapped for show in front of an audience. Today mummies are seldom unwrapped, and always by archaeologists for serious study.

The mummy of a palace official, c. 725 BC.

Mummies were buried in one or more coffins that were human in shape and painted with a face to resemble the person inside. The coffins were also decorated with pictures and hieroglyphs that showed the afterlife or explained who the dead person was, what their job had been, and sometimes who their family were.

X-RAYS AND SCANNING TECHNIQUES

The need to unwrap mummies became much less after the invention of X-rays in 1895. X-rays of mummies have revealed some surprising secrets beneath the bandages. The mummy of a child was found to include the bones of a cat, and the mummy of a princess had two heads packed inside it. This suggests that embalmers were not above using one embalming job to tidy up the leftovers of an earlier one!

CT scans are where a mummy is X-rayed several times in cross section to build up a picture of all the layers of wrapping.

A mummy inside its painted coffin about to undergo a CT scan. The scanner is on the left. CT scans allow archaeologists to learn about mummies without risking the damage that might be caused by opening their coffins and exposing them to the air.

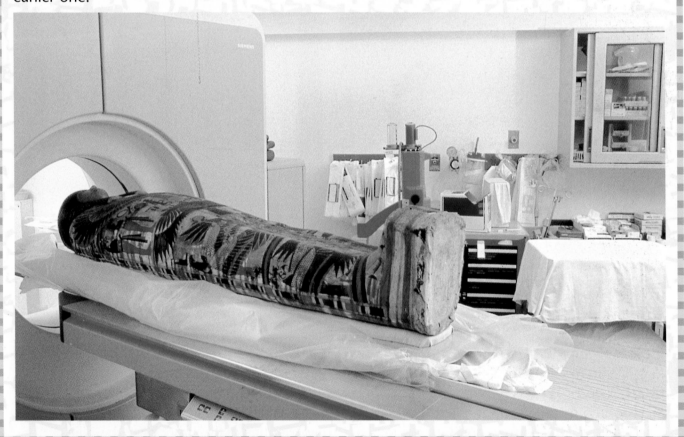

CLUES FROM THE DEAD

Mummies tell us a lot about the embalming process, and also provide clues about religion in ancient Egypt, but what do they tell us about the people inside the bandages? The answer is, quite a lot.

Egyptologists can work out how important people were from where they were buried and how grand their tombs were. Examining the bodies reveals how old they were when they died, their sex, how tall they were, what colour their hair was and even if they bit their nails! Sometimes it is even possible to tell if a person died naturally or from disease, illness or in battle.

A scientist conducts forensic tests on a sample of hair taken from the mummy of an Egyptian woman.

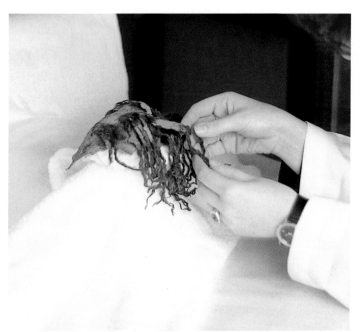
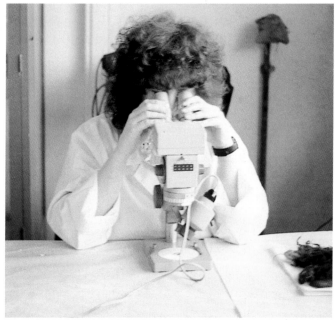

FORENSIC TECHNIQUES

One of the first archaeologists to use forensic techniques similar to those that the police use to solve a murder was Armand Ruffer. In 1909 he found that you could soak mummified tissue in a mixture of alcohol and bicarbonate of soda to examine it. He discovered that fishermen and farmers in ancient Egypt, who worked in or near the River Nile, often suffered from 'bilharzia'. This is caused by small worms that bore into the feet. Once inside the body they breed and feed, causing damage to the internal organs and even death. Bilharzia still affects modern-day Egyptians who work near the Nile.

A FACE FROM THE PAST

Richard Neave, who makes facial reconstructions for the police and for archaeologists, reconstructed the face of Natsef-Amun, a mummified ancient Egyptian priest. He used CT scans to make a replica of the skull with a computer controlled machine. This meant that the replica was very accurate.

The 'fleshing out' of the face was based on the bone structure of the skull and known forensic details about the thickness of skin and muscle on a human face. Natsef-Amun's nose was broad and his upper and lower jaw jutted out strongly. His face, when the skin and muscle layers had been added, strongly suggested African ancestry. He came from Upper Egypt, where many people from Nubia (modern Sudan) had settled.

The only piece of real guesswork in the reconstruction was the level of wrinkling on the face, based on the fact that Natsef-Amun was middle-aged when he died.

Richard Neave's reconstruction of Natsef-Amun's face.

FINDING TUTANKHAMUN

The most famous ancient Egyptian of all is the pharaoh Tutankhamun. Why? Not for being a particularly good ruler, or even a long-lived one. We know very little about his short, nine-year reign. He is famous because of the treasure that Egyptologists found in his tomb. The tomb had been robbed by the ancient Egyptians, but much of the treasure had been left behind and had remained untouched ever since.

WHO WAS TUTANKHAMUN?

Tutankhamun was the son of the pharaoh Akhenaten, and became pharaoh in 1336 BC, aged 8 or 9. Tutankhamun married but had no living children to rule after him (the mummies of two children who died at birth were found in his tomb).

Just some of the furniture and equipment in Tutankhamun's tomb, ransacked by ancient Egyptian tomb robbers in their search for portable valuables.

We do not know how Tutankhamun died, but his death must have been sudden and unexpected: his tomb is small for a pharaoh and only one room has painted walls. Some of his grave goods seem to have been made for someone else too.

HOWARD CARTER

Tutankhamun's tomb was discovered by the archaeologist Howard Carter. In 1907 he began to work for Lord Carnarvon and was given a permit to excavate in the Valley of the Kings. By 1922 little had been found and Carter had to beg Carnarvon to fund one more excavation. If nothing was found, Carter promised to repay Carnarvon's money. That year, just days after work had begun, they found Tutankhamun's tomb.

Howard Carter and an assistant at work on Tutankhamun's mummy.

THE TREASURE OF TUTANKHAMUN

Tutankhamun's treasure filled four rooms. When Carter found it, it was clear that the tomb had been robbed in ancient times. Many small objects such as jewellery and perfumes were gone. Carter found eight rings tied in a hankie, dropped as the robbers had left.

But the larger objects remained. Most importantly, the mummy had not been touched at all. It was still inside three mummy cases, a stone coffin (sarcophagus) and four outer boxes, all covered in gold decoration. When these were all opened, Carter's team found the death mask of the pharaoh. It was made from solid gold and weighed 10.25 kilogrammes.

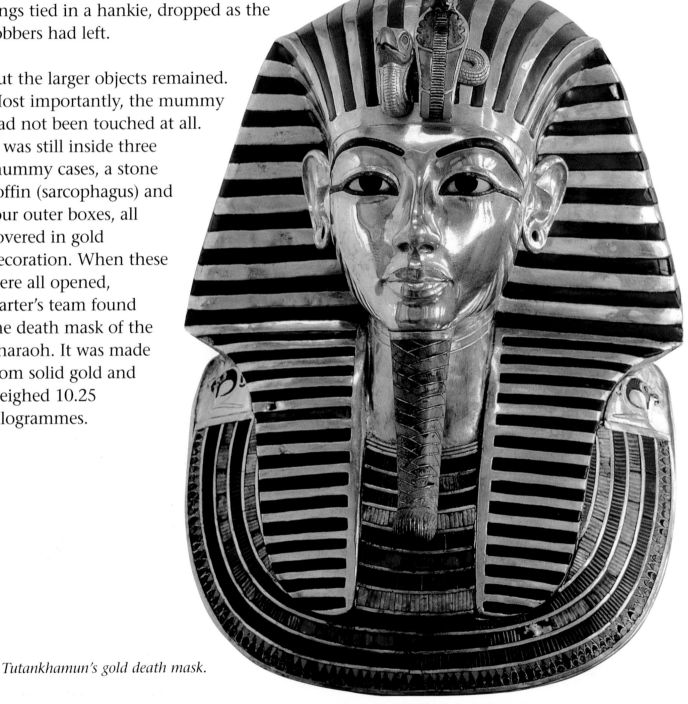

Tutankhamun's gold death mask.

PROJECT: MAKE TUTANKHAMUN'S NECKLACE

1. Copy or trace the design of the bottom part of the necklace shown below onto a piece of thin card and cut it out.

2. Glue coloured paper and foil wrappers onto the design, cut to fit each section, or simply colour it in, as shown in the example below. Look carefully at the photograph of the real necklace on the right to give you ideas.

3. Cut a length of gold wrapping ribbon or thread long enough to go round your neck, and glue the ends to each side of your ancient Egyptian necklace. Don't wear the necklace until the glue has dried!

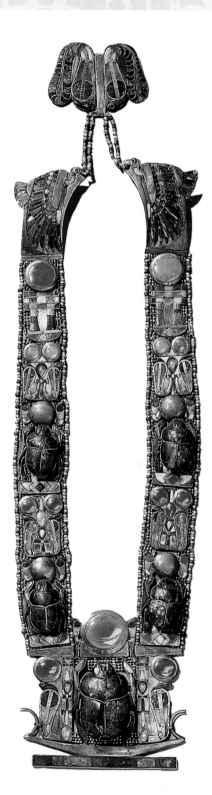

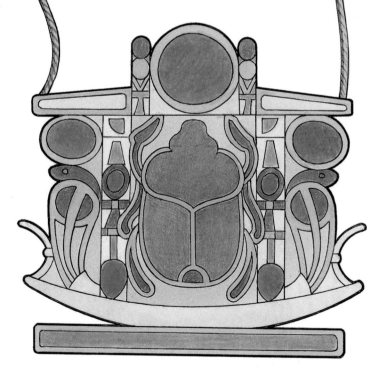

Tutankhamun's magnificent necklace.

TEMPLES AND STATUES

The huge stone temples that the ancient Egyptians built to their gods and goddesses give archaeologists a lot of clues about the beliefs and customs of the time.

Some gods and goddesses, like Amun and Hathor, had larger temples than other gods. This suggests that they were more important. Some gods were only important in certain places. Sobek, the crocodile god, for example, had his main temple on the banks of the River Nile at Kom Ombo in southern Egypt, and another at Shedyet, also on the Nile.

Luxor temple, where Amun was worshipped. Amun was the most important of the ancient Egyptian gods, and so had the biggest and most impressive temples.

WHAT HAPPENED IN THE TEMPLES?

Temples were not like modern churches. Written evidence shows that ordinary people were not allowed into them. Only priests and the pharaoh were allowed in, to perform religious rituals and care for the statue of the god. As the priests got closer to the room where the god was kept, fewer and fewer of them were allowed to go any further. Only the high priest of the temple could handle the statue of the god.

The largest temple sites had a palace for the pharaoh to stay in when he visited, and a complex of rooms for the priests and officials. Large temples such as the temple of Horus at Edfu have shown that they also had store-rooms, a library, a school room and a sacred lake where the priests had to bathe before entering the temple.

HERODOTUS

One of the first tourists in Egypt was the ancient Greek writer Herodotus in 450 BC. He wrote about his visit, describing the country and the people, the priests and their rituals. He saw the temple complex at Shedyet, home of the crocodile god Sobek:

'The City of the Crocodiles is more amazing than the pyramids. It has twelve covered courtyards surrounded by a huge wall. There are about three thousand rooms, half of which are underground. I saw the upper rooms, and it is hard to believe that men built them. They were built of stone and covered with beautiful figures.'

A statue of Sobek, the crocodile god.

MAKING SENSE OF TEMPLE REMAINS

It can be hard for Egyptologists to understand temple sites, and even harder for ordinary visitors. They are a jumble of stone walls, ramps and broken pillars, covered in hieroglyphs and carvings. In ancient times the walls and pillars would have been painted in bright colours, with gold, silver and precious stones decorating the more important parts. Some areas were roofed over, others open to the sky.

Egyptologists can draw detailed plans and diagrams of what these places might have been like, but even these do not bring them to life. Modern computer technology has changed all this. Computers are now used to help archaeologists reconstruct what temples, pyramids and even whole towns might have looked like.

Some archaeologists believe that a 'try it and see' approach can help them to understand temple and other sites. They have tried to test out their ideas about building techniques by constructing pyramids on a small scale, using the techniques they think the ancient Egyptians used. Techniques tested in this way have been used to make repairs at several temple sites.

Egyptologists excavate a temple site.

STATUES

The huge statues of the pharaohs and gods tell archaeologists how important these beings were. They also show that, despite the evidence of tomb paintings and models, the ancient Egyptians understood proportion very well, and were able to keep to proportion even when working on a huge scale.

Ancient Egyptian statue-makers did not always work on a huge scale. They also made small statues from wood, precious metals, and stone. These statues were most often of gods and goddesses, often showing them as animals – a hippo is the goddess Tawaret, a cat the goddess Bast.

RADIOGRAPHY

Radiographic techniques have helped archaeologists to discover where the stone used for some statues came from. For example a small sample of the stone from the two colossi of Memnon was powdered and given a dose of radiation, and the time it took for the radiation to decay was measured. Then the decay-rate of stone from various quarries was measured until a match was found.

These Egyptologists are measuring a statue in the huge temple of Amun.

TOWNS

Almost all ancient Egyptian settlements were built along the River Nile, close to the farmland that the annual flooding of the river made fertile. Although the Nile does not flood any more, thanks to dams built at Aswan, people in modern Egypt still tend to live close to the river. This means that most ancient Egyptian settlements are underneath modern ones.

Many modern Egyptian houses are still made from mud brick.

Excavations at three towns, Tell el-Amarna, Kahun and Deir el-Medina have shown that ordinary homes were made from mud brick and painted inside, often with simple patterns decorating the walls. They had wooden doors and shutters and most had earth floors, although the houses at Deir el-Medina, in the desert, had stone floors. All homes were like this, even those of important people. The only buildings made from stone were tombs and temples. Even royal palaces, like that of the pharaoh Amenhotep III at Malkata, were built using mud brick.

Important people had bigger homes. The walls had more complicated wall paintings and these houses also had gardens where people could sit in the shade of trees. Ordinary people just had small yards, and probably sat on the flat roof under cloth awnings, as they still do today. They may have cooked there too.

AKHENATEN, HERETIC PHARAOH

Continuing with ideas first introduced by his father Amenhotep III, Akhenaten changed the religion of his country from the worship of many gods to worshipping just one: Aten, the sun god. Because the pharaoh was also chief priest, he was allowed to do this. But not everyone obeyed. People who accepted the new religion went with him to his new city of Tell el-Amarna, which at its height had between 20–50,000 people living there. However, many of those who did not go with him carried on with the old ways. Because Egypt is a long, thin country, it could take over two weeks to reach the new city from the old settlements, and as the pharaoh seldom 'toured' his lands, he probably never knew he was being disobeyed. After Akhenaten died, people drifted back to Thebes and Akhenaten's new religion died out. Later pharaohs had his city destroyed and his statues smashed.

A statue of Akhenaten, made during his reign. It shows the style of art he favoured, which gave people longer faces and tubby stomachs!

KAHUN

The labourers who built the pyramid of Sesostris II at Lahun (in about 1895 BC) lived in Kahun, a village built especially for them. It was close enough to the Nile for them to have farmland nearby to grow their own food.

Kahun was surrounded by a wall and had over 100 homes for workers and their families, as well as larger houses for the architects and overseers. There was one very large building with high walls, big rooms, courtyards and gardens. Egyptologists think that the pharaoh may have stayed here when he visited the site to check that his tomb was being built properly.

Excavations at Kahun uncovered a wide variety of ordinary tools and equipment, which told Egyptologists a great deal about how workers made things. They found metal and stone tools, showing an overlap of stone- and bronze-age technology. They also found moulds that showed how the metal tools were made, as well as moulds for making mud bricks, with the mud still stuck to them.

Part of a Middle Kingdom papyrus picture showing an ancient Egyptian mud brick house, painted white.

AERIAL ARCHAEOLOGY

The desert sands of Egypt, while preserving artefacts very well, have always made life difficult for Egyptologists because they quickly bury the evidence and make even the remains of towns very hard to find. Today this is made easier by using photographs taken from satellites and balloons, which can be enlarged so that very small areas can be studied.

DEIR EL-MEDINA

Deir el-Medina was built for the families of the men working on the tombs in the Valley of the Kings. Unlike at Kahun, the workers at Deir el-Medina did not have fields to farm. All their food and water was transported to the town by donkey. Workers and their families lived in about 70 mud brick terraced houses on either side of a main street, inside a mud brick wall. Each house had four rooms, with stone floors and wooden doors. There were no windows – light came through slots in the flat roofs. A few larger houses were found, probably for the overseers, but no really large houses and no palace.

Egyptologists found some tools at Deir el-Medina, but the most important finds were the tombs that the workers had built for *themselves*. Documents found here show exactly how the workers organized themselves and what daily life in the town was like. The records show that the workers were paid in bread, beer, oil and linen. They list the days when they worked, the days they rested, and the reasons they had time off (two reasons given were religious festivals and time for brewing the family beer).

The excavated stone foundations of the houses at Deir el-Medina. The 'plan' of the town can clearly be seen.

PRESERVING THE PAST

Archaeologists want to find out about the past hidden beneath our feet, and until recently the only way to do this has been to excavate. But as soon as archaeologists uncover ancient artefacts and buildings, exposing them to different conditions, they begin to decay, and are also likely to be damaged each time they are handled.

So, as soon as an artefact or building is uncovered, archaeologists have to try to preserve it. One solution is to take objects to a museum as quickly as possible, but this causes its own problems. The museum in Cairo is close to the Nile, so the air is damper than in the desert. Even in glass cases, artefacts from the Valley of the Kings are exposed to daylight and the damper air.

The inner court of the Cairo Museum, where smaller artefacts are displayed in glass cases.

THE CLIMATE OF EGYPT: A BLESSING AND A CURSE

The dry climate of the Egyptian desert has helped to preserve things far better than the damp soils of cooler, wetter countries. Without the dry, hot sand to protect them, no wooden objects from the time of the pharaohs would have survived at all. The climate is so dry that it has also preserved food such as bread, meat and fruit. On the other hand the extreme heat of the days and the very cold nights cause the stone of tombs, statues and temples to expand and contract, and cracks can develop.

In 1955 one of the shoulders of the Sphinx gave way and was repaired with stone as close as possible to the original stone. But the builders used modern techniques and secured the shoulder with mortar. As a result the shoulder soon began to shift, and was pushing the Sphinx out of line. Recent restoration has now cured the problem.

Restoration work on the legs of the Sphinx. Egyptologists have constantly to face the question of what will do ancient structures more harm: leaving them alone and letting the weather wear them away, or trying to repair them and perhaps damage them in the process.

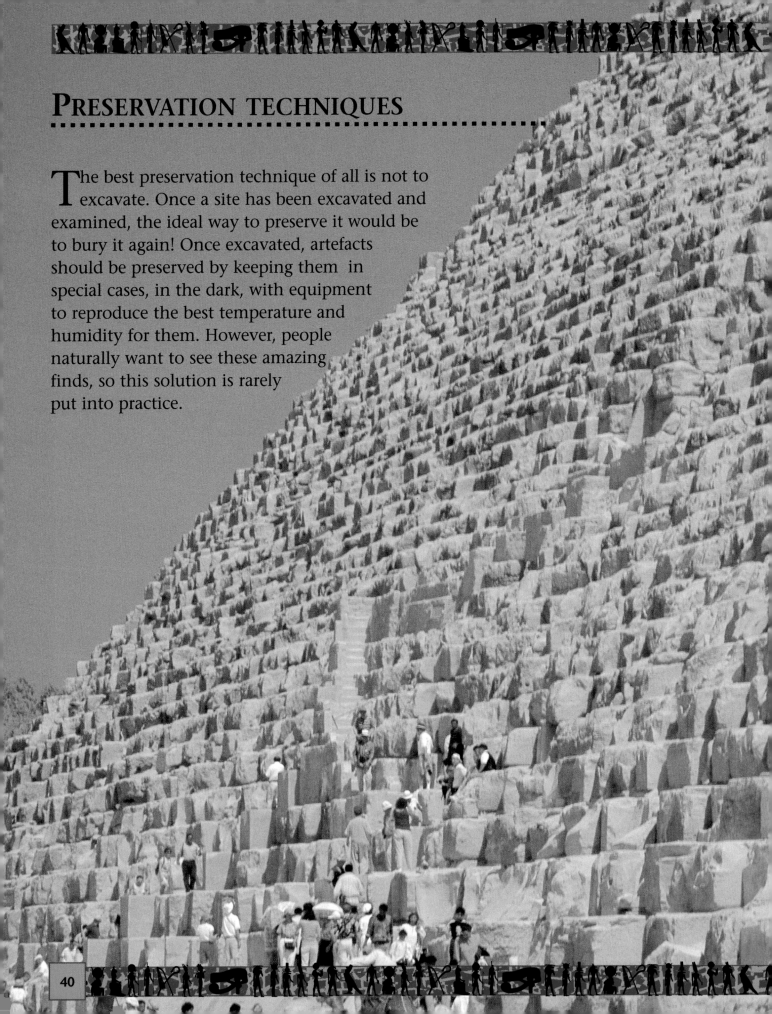

PRESERVATION TECHNIQUES

The best preservation technique of all is not to excavate. Once a site has been excavated and examined, the ideal way to preserve it would be to bury it again! Once excavated, artefacts should be preserved by keeping them in special cases, in the dark, with equipment to reproduce the best temperature and humidity for them. However, people naturally want to see these amazing finds, so this solution is rarely put into practice.

Wear and tear can be reduced by limiting the number of people who visit monuments and making sure that visitors are not allowed to touch them or climb on them. Some archaeologists think that the famous 'lost nose' of the Sphinx was caused by people climbing the monument. The Sphinx's beard has also fallen off, and part of it is now on display in the British Museum.

Keeping a careful eye on visitors also helps to stop the worst damage that they can do: taking away a 'small piece' of the past to keep as a souvenir. With thousands of visitors every year, if everyone was tempted to take even a small piece of rock from Egypt's pyramids, temples and tombs, they would quickly disappear!

Even the best behaved of visitors to a site cause damage unintentionally: just by walking, sweating and breathing. Walking wears away floors; sweating and breathing inside tombs increases the humidity and can cause the wall paintings gradually to flake away.

The tomb of Horemheb, pharaoh from 1321–1295 BC, attracts thousands of visitors every year, with the result that the wall paintings are being damaged.

For hundreds of years, visitors have wanted to climb the pyramids. This has caused a great deal of wear and tear.

WHAT NEXT?

Archaeologists are constantly looking for new techniques to help them find out more about the past without disturbing sites too much. They use techniques and machines first developed for the engineering industry, forensic science and medicine. Several new inventions suggest that archaeology will become even more exciting and 'artefact friendly' in the future.

Computer generated images of the skull and head of a female Egyptian mummy. Modern techniques like this are helping to revolutionize archaeology.

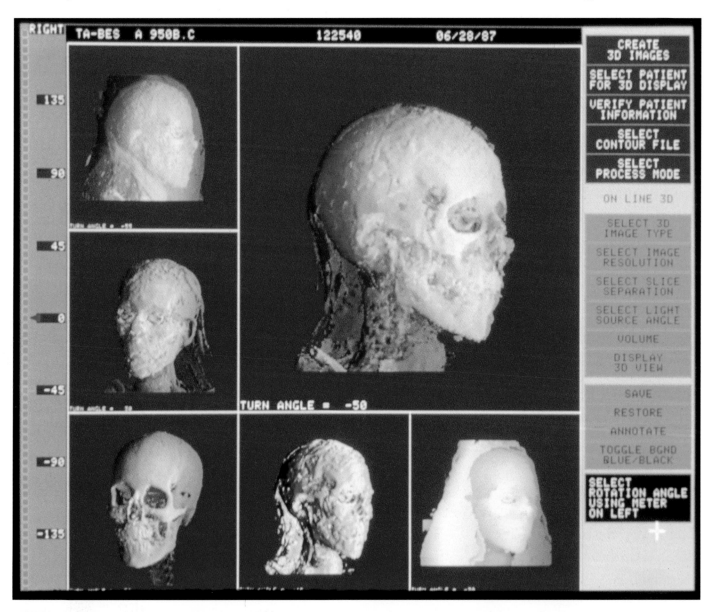

BRINGING THE PAST BACK TO LIFE

DNA is the genetic material of every living cell. In 1984 Svante Pääbo, a Swedish scientist, took samples from 23 mummies and found cells in the leg of a mummified child with intact DNA. When more DNA has been extracted from mummies, Egyptologists may be able to work out the family links between all the ancient Egyptians, and even who their Neanderthal ancestors were. It might even be possible to use DNA to clone an ancient Egyptian person. However, at present it is just an idea, and there are many physical, technological and moral problems to sort out before this could even be attempted.

Today, archaeologists can examine underground sites without excavating, and store the information on a computer. They can also feed computers information and produce an image of what the site would have looked like. The latest virtual reality techniques, used with ground penetration radar and other underground scanning equipment, allow archaeologists to 'excavate' and 're-create' a site that they can explore on-screen as if they were there.

Such technology is an archaeologist's dream: it allows a site to be investigated and then explored while preserving it completely, because it is never even dug up.

Not all archaeology in the future will rely on the latest technology because archaeological projects are very often short of money. Sometimes there is not enough time to do anything other than a basic dig. For example, 'rescue archaeology', which is done against the clock in the path of diggers making a new road, farmers making new fields, or on sites uncovered during building works. There will always be a place for 'traditional' excavation, using hand tools and willing helpers.

Most modern-day excavations in Egypt still use traditional methods, such as the slow and careful scraping away of sand, shown here.

TIMELINES

ANCIENT EGYPTIAN TIMELINE (ALL DATES ARE BC)

Different Egyptologists use different dating systems when referring to ancient Egypt.

25000	12000	3500	3100	2686–2181
First settlements along the River Nile	First farming along the Nile	First mummies?	Upper and Lower Egypt are united by the pharaoh Narmer	**Old Kingdom**

1650–1550	1550–1069	1352–1336	1350–1336	1336–1327
Second Intermediate Period Different parts of Egypt were ruled by different kings and governors. Some of these groups fought among themselves.	**New Kingdom** Royals and important people were buried in the Valley of the Kings. Workmen lived in the town of Deir el-Medina (see pages 14–15,37).	Akhenaten pharaoh (see page 35)	Tell el-Amarna flourished (see page 35)	Tutankhamun pharaoh (see pages 26–29)

ARCHAEOLOGICAL TIMELINE (ALL DATES ARE AD)

1799	1816–1821	1822	1832	1888–1889	1894
Rosetta Stone discovered (see page 20)	Belzoni 'excavating' in Egypt (see page 7)	Champollion reveals the meaning of hieroglyphs (see pages 20–21)	Champollion finishes his hieroglyph word list and dictionary (see pages 20–21)	Flinders Petrie begins to excavate Lahun and Kahun (see pages 9 and 36)	Petrie begins to use the technique of stratification (see page 9)

The system used here is the one used by the British Museum.

2650–2400	2558–2532	2181–2055	2055–1650	1880
Great age of pyramid building (see pages 10–13)	Khafra pharaoh and Sphinx built (see page 13)	**First Intermediate Period** Different parts of Egypt were ruled by different kings and governors. Some of these groups fought among themselves.	**Middle Kingdom**	Town of Kahun constructed to house workers building the pyramid complex at Lahun (see page 36)

1069–747	747–332	450	30
Third Intermediate Period Different parts of Egypt were ruled by different kings and governors. Some of these groups fought among themselves.	**Late Period**	The Greek writer Herodotus visited Egypt (see page 31)	Egypt becomes part of the Roman Empire after the death of Cleopatra

1899	1903–1914	1922	1984	1990	1997
Petrie finds the remains of Zer, the first royal mummy (see page 9)	Theodore Davis excavating in the Valley of the Kings (see page 14)	Howard Carter discovers Tutankhamun's tomb (see pages 26–29)	Svante Pääbo extracts the DNA of a mummy (see page 43)	Richard Neave reconstructs the face of Egyptian priest Natsef-Amun (see page 25)	Earliest mummies yet discovered found at Hierakonpolis (see page 8)

GLOSSARY

amulet a small ornament, often representing a god or goddess, worn to protect a person (even dead people) from evil.

archaeologist a person who looks for and studies things that have survived from past times.

architect a person who designs buildings.

artefact something that a person has made.

demotic day-to-day Egyptian language developed from hieratic.

Egyptologist a person who studies ancient Egypt.

embalm to preserve a dead body from decay.

excavate to dig systematically in order to carefully explore a site.

forensic science 'forensic' actually means 'of or used in courts of law', and forensic science refers to scientific techniques used to obtain evidence in criminal investigations. These techniques, such as chemical analysis, are used by archaeologists to examine human remains, clothing fragments etc.

hieratic a simple form of hieroglyphs, used for letters and everyday writing.

hieroglyphs writing that uses pictures and symbols rather than letters to represent sounds or whole words.

humidity the amount of water there is in the air.

linen cloth made from spinning and weaving the fibres of the flax plant.

natron a form of salt, mostly made up of sodium carbonate and sodium bicarbonate, used by embalmers to dry out bodies ready for mummification.

Neanderthal man an extinct race of people who lived in Europe, Africa and Asia between about 115,000 and 40,000 years ago.

Nubia a region of north-east Africa between Egypt and Sudan. Much of Nubia is now drowned by Lake Nasser. From about 2000 BC the Egyptians occupied Nubia, which they called Kush.

overseer a person in charge of a group of workers.

pharaoh a king of ancient Egypt.

shabti a statue of a worker, placed into a tomb to work for the dead person in the afterlife.

FURTHER INFORMATION

PLACES TO VISIT

Britain
The Pitt-Rivers Museum
South Parks Road
Oxford
OX1 3PP

Egypt
The Egyptian Museum
Tahrir Square
Cairo

USA
The Metropolitan Museum
1000 Fifth Avenue at 82nd
Street

BOOKS

Builders and Craftsmen
(Ancient Egypt series)
by Jane Shuter
(Heinemann, 1999)

Discoveries and Inventions
(Ancient Egypt series)
by Jane Shuter
(Heinemann, 1998)

*Men, Woman and Children
in Ancient Egypt*
by Jane Bingham
(Wayland, 2007)

*In the Daily Life of the Ancient
Egyptians*
(Gods and Goddesses series)
by Henrietta McCall
(Wayland, 2002)

CLUBS

The Young Archaeologist's
Club,
St Mary's House
66 Bootham
YO30 7BZ

Use this book for teaching literacy

This book can help you in the literacy hour in the following ways:

 Children can read and evaluate the projects in this book for their purpose, organisation and clarity. (Year 5: Understanding and interpreting texts)

 They can use this book to collect, define and spell technical words used by archaeologists or historians. (Year 5: Word structure and spelling)

 The book is an example of an explanatory text in which children can investigate and note features of impersonal style. (Year 5: Understanding and interpreting texts)

 The discussion contained in chapters 12 and 13 can be used by children to draft and write letters of their own arguing the case for preserving the past for future generations. (Year 5: Creating and shaping texts)

INDEX

Numbers in **bold** refer to picture captions